INSIDE HISTORY
Castle

Illustrated by Peter Dennis

W
FRANKLIN WATTS
LONDON • SYDNEY

Contents

Medieval castles

Castles are found all over the world, but they all have one thing in common. They were built by rich and powerful people, such as knights, kings or wealthy landowners, to defend and control the land around them. Castles were homes for a lord and his family and his guards. Among the other castle-dwellers were cooks and domestic servants, knights and their pages and squires, blacksmiths, carpenters, grooms and priests. There might also be minstrels and jesters to keep the lord amused. Overseeing all the castle activities was the steward.

In Europe, the earliest castles were little more than wooden forts, usually built on the top of a hill, called a motte. Sometimes there would be a small settlement next to the fort in an enclosure, called a bailey. Eventually, the wooden forts were replaced by stone buildings. These were much stronger and easier to defend. Called keeps or donjons, they were simply stone towers, with high walls and small windows.

As time went on, castles needed even stronger defences. These included a moat or ditch surrounding the castle, crossed by a drawbridge that could be raised when attackers approached. Thick walls were also built around castles, making it even more difficult for attackers to gain entry. Despite these measures, a long siege with special weapons could eventually bring down even the strongest of castles.

Block and tackle winching up building stones

A LUXURY HOME

This castle is not only a fortress to protect the lord, his family and people from attack, but also a symbol of the lord's great wealth and importance. It is a home too, and will have luxurious rooms for the lord's family to live in.

Fixing roof timbers

Laying roof tiles

Rubble infill

Master mason

Chapel

Digging the well

Quarrying building stone on-site

Using scaffolding to reach up the walls

Crane

Measuring

ROOF MATERIALS
Thatch is the cheapest roofing material, but it can very easily catch fire. Thin, flat squares of wood called shingles are easy to make, but they rot and also burn easily. A castle of this quality will use pottery tiles. These are fireproof and longlasting.

Holes to support roof beams

Fixing the roof beams

Limewashing

Filling in gaps between the stone blocks with mortar

BUILDING WORKERS

Building a castle of this size needs hundreds of workers. As well as labourers there would be sawyers to cut up the wood, carpenters and joiners to fix the woodwork, plasterers, painters, roofers, tilers and masons.

Laying floorboards

Painting the chapel

Laying tiles

Plastering walls

Digging the well

Laying down flagstones on the passageway floor

MASTER MASON
The master mason is in charge of the building of the castle. His is very well paid by the lord for his services. He is in charge of the free masons—skilled craftsmen who cut and carve the building stones.

Building the castle

The lord of this castle has chosen a good site to build on. It is on raised ground with a good view across the land from all sides. There is a well within the castle walls to supply castle dwellers with fresh water. Building the castle will take several years. It is being constructed out of local stone from nearby quarries and timber from the surrounding forest.

Treadmill: used to power the crane

Play fighting

Constructing an arch

Plastering walls

Bringing in equipment and supplies

Breaking up quarry stone into blocks

Spiral staircase

Wooden shutters cover crenelles—spaces from where archers can shoot arrows.

CHAPEL

The lord and his family will worship here several times a day. The chapel's beautiful stained glass windows are a sign of the lord's great wealth.

Chimney

Merlons: high sections between crenelles

Great Hall

Machicolations: overhanging stone structures through which guards can shoot attackers below

Stained glass windows

Well

Roofs covered in pottery tiles

Chapel

CRENELLATIONS

The castle has been very sturdily built. It is well defended with strong walls topped by crenellations—jagged battlements with gaps, called crenelles, for archers to fire through. The lord had to get a special licence from the king to add these battlements to his castle. It is these that make castles different from any other building. If the lord had built the castle without the licence, the king could have seized it from him.

Garderobe or latrine

THICK WALLS

The walls between towers are called curtain walls. To strengthen them, they have been built up to two metres thick. The outer and inner surfaces are made of stone blocks and the

Lord's standard

Crenellations

GREAT HALL

At the centre of the castle is the Great Hall. The lord carries out much of his business here. Meals are served in it too, and a fire is kept burning all year round. Many of the castle servants sleep in the Great Hall at night.

Wall walk

Limewashed walls

Arrow slit

gap between them infilled with rocks and mortar—a mixture of sand, lime and water. The walls are then limewashed (painted white) to protect against the rain and to give a smart finish.

ARROW SLITS

Narrow holes in the castle walls allow archers to shoot out, but it is almost impossible for the enemy to shoot back through them.

ALCHEMIST

Alchemists believe it is possible to turn ordinary metals into gold. They also try to find an "elixir of life" that will cure all human ills.

Alchemist

Minstrels

Servants' bedchamber

Roasting meat

The lord and lady dining in the Great Hall

Kitchens

Steward's office

Praying in the chapel

Guardsmen passing the time by playing dice

The garderobe (latrine) empties into the moat or ditch below.

The core of the wall is filled with rubble and mortar.

Gunpowder store

Bedchamber

KITCHENS

One of the busiest and largest areas of the castle is the kitchens. The cooks, bakers, scullions and other kitchen servants work day and night to keep everyone in the castle fed. It's even busier here at feast times.

Armourer making chain mail

Play fighting

Crossbowmen on watch duty

Battlements

Castle life

The castle was completed a few years ago now, and life inside has settled into a routine. Many people are needed to keep the castle running smoothly—there is always plenty going on within its walls. The castle has never been attacked, but the lord insists his guards keep a careful look out, just in case.

Drawbridge supports

A messenger approaches the castle bearing a letter for the lord.

Oubliette: A small cell beneath the dungeon floor

Raised portcullis

Stone spiral staircase inside tower

Tournament

To keep his knights busy and to test their fighting skills, the lord has decided to hold a tournament. Here knights will fight mock battles, called melees, and joust against each other on horseback. In the joust, knights try to unhorse their opponents by charging at them with a long wooden lances. Points are gained for breaking your lance on your opponent's shield.

COATS OF ARMS

Before the joust all the knights parade in front of the audience, who cheer for their favourites. Because they are wearing armour, it is impossible to tell which knight is which. So the competitors and their horses wear distinctively patterned colours, and the knights carry shields decorated with their coats of arms. This way they can be easily recognized from a distance.

The lord and lady and their guests watch from a raised stand.

Tilt

Jousting knights

Standard

Squires ready to assist their knights

Tent where knights change into their armour

Castle

Ladies watching
the melee

Judges

Knights waiting to
begin the melee

Practising hand-to-
hand fighting

Shattered
lance

Melee

Squire

Knight

THE MELEE
During a melee, knights rush at each other and try to knock off each other's helmets. Their squires wait at the side in case the knights need any help.

Herald

Minstrels

FINE BUILDINGS

The grandest building in the town is the stone-built church at its centre. This has been built not for worship, but to show the world how prosperous the town and the lord are. When he built his castle the lord made lots of changes to the church as well. He made it bigger and added a tall spire and many impressive stone carvings. Some of the finer buildings in the town, such as the rich merchant's house, are built of expensive stone. The poorer houses are made from cheaper timber with walls of sticks and plaster, called wattle and daub.

WINDMILL

The windmill is owned by the lord. All the farmers on his land must bring their grain to be ground into flour here. The lord charges them a fee for this, called multure. When the mill is not working the miller positions the sails in a diagonal cross to signal to the farmers not to come and save them a wasted journey.

Castle

Gatehouse entrance to town

Church

Timber-framed houses

Wattle and daub walls

Belfry

Windmill

CROWDED HOUSES

The town's buildings contain shops and workshops on the ground floor with living areas above. Rich men, such as wine merchants, may own a whole house and let part of it out for others to live in. Poorer people may occupy just one small room near the top of the building.

Artist's studio

Poor family

Four-poster bed

Merchant's house

Merchant's wife

Taking sheep to market

Baker

Tailor

DISEASE!

Diseases are common in medieval towns. People live crowded together and there is no running water. Bubonic plague is particularly feared. It is a deadly disease carried by rat fleas that arrives with the warmer weather. It is much feared, as there is no known cure and many people die of it. Leprosy is another dreaded sickness. Sufferers, called lepers, are made to carry a bell to warn of their approach.

Collecting the bodies of plague victims

MEDIEVAL MARKET

Market day is the busiest day of the week for a medieval town. Local farmers come to sell meat and vegetables. Travelling merchants come from afar to sell their fine cloth and other wares. Pedlars sell all sorts of goods from ribbons and bows to pins and needles. Tinkers will repair pots and pans, while jugglers, jesters and even dancing bears entertain the crowds.

CRAFTSMEN

Many different craftsmen work in the town, including leatherworkers, silversmiths, tailors and an armourer. Craftsmen form themselves into societies, called guilds, which lay down rules about how they go about their work. There is also an artist in the town. He makes a living by painting portraits of the rich.

The windmill's sails turn heavy mill stones which grind the grain into flour.

In the town

Below the castle lies a thriving market town. The lord of the castle owns some of the town's buildings, including the windmill. While most of the townsfolk are poor, there are some very wealthy citizens living here too. A rich wine merchant, for instance, has built a large house in the centre of the town.

Ringing the church bell

Scholar

Rich merchant's rooms

Plague victim

Armourer

Wine cellar

Leper

Knight with his squire

Tiled roofs
smashed by
enemy missiles

CANNONS

Before the invention
of cannons, it was
very difficult to
smash through thick
castle walls. But
cannonballs can
easily blast through
tiled roofs and
sometimes even
thick stone walls.
This means that
castles are not the
secure fortresses
they once were.

BATTERING RAM

Battering rams are made
from a heavy tree trunk
suspended within a frame.
This can than be swung
with great force to smash
down barriers. Once the
gatehouse entrance has
been destroyed, the
attackers can swarm
inside the castle.

Battering ram
protected inside
a covered
wooden frame

Drawbridge
pulled up to act
as barrier

Gatehouse
entrance
destroyed by
battering ram

Enemy
cannon

Throwing a
fire bomb

Animal
hides help
reduce the
spread of
fire

A siege tower
allows the enemy
to gain access to
the top of the
castle walls.

Smooth sloping
tower walls are
difficult to climb.

Shooting crossbows and long bows through arrow slits in the castle wall

Crossbowmen

Pouring hot sand on to the enemy through a murder hole

Battering ram made out of a sturdy tree trunk

Infilled ditch

Siege!

It is a few weeks since the tournament and the castle's defences are finally being tested. A dispute with a neighbouring lord has erupted into open war. The rival lord besieged the castle, and when it refused to surrender he ordered his men to attack. The castle's lord is determined not to give in. The knights and soldiers are well trained and everyone is fighting hard to defeat the attackers. But as the enemy are well equipped, it is going to be a fierce contest.

An enemy fire bomb flung by a giant catapult, called a trebuchet, finds its mark.

Enemy soldiers inside the siege tower

Brazier to heat up oil and sand

Murder hole

Winding a crossbow ready to fire

Carrying water to douse the fire

Enemy soldiers fire guns and shoot crossbows from behind wooden shields called mantlets.

RESTORATION

Several hundred years of neglect left the castle very unsafe. Restoration work has repaired a lot of the damage. Some parts have been left as ruins, but they have been made safe for visitors to explore.

Remains of the alchemist's turret

Exploring the ruined battlements

Hole made by cannonball

New steps and walkway

A modern lead roof has replaced the damaged tiles.

Actors recreating a medieval combat

Old moat

Walkway

Advertising an event at the castle

Archaeologists excavate the stone quarry in front of the castle.

HISTORICAL HERITAGE

Looking after the ruins of buildings like this castle is an expensive business. It requires a lot of skill and knowledge. But many people believe the expense is very worthwhile. It gives visitors the chance to explore historical buildings and discover what it was like to live in such places many hundreds of years ago.

Holes in the wall that held roof joists are still visible.

Television crew

CLUES TO THE PAST

Archaeologists working at this castle site have found many objects, such as belt buckles and bits of armour, from medieval times. These can help us understand how people lived 600 years ago.

Guided tour

Great Hall

Cinema

Café

Model of the castle

Well

Passageway

Excavation

VISITOR ATTRACTION

There is much for visitors to see in the castle now. Some of the rooms, like the lord's bedchamber, have been completely restored. Other areas have been converted into museum, shop and exhibition areas. Actors dressed as medieval people bring the castle back to life.

Castle ruins today

The attack on the castle was successful, and the badly damaged castle gradually fell into ruin. Today, centuries later, it has been partially restored so that visitors can get a glimpse of what it might have been like to live in medieval times.

Restored bedchamber

Weapons display

Ruined towers

Battlements

Car park

Restored tower

Museum display

Ghost!

Oubliette

Shop

Entrance kiosk

Glossary

Arrow slit (*above*) An opening in a castle wall through which arrows were shot.

Battering ram A large tree trunk used to break down walls or doors.

Battlements The top of a wall with a series of gaps (crenelles) between raised portions (merlons). They are also called crenellations.

Coat of arms (*top right*) The emblem of a noble family, usually in the shape of a decorated shield.

Crenellations *see* battlements.

Crossbow A mechanical bow using short bolts rather than arrows.

Garderobe A toilet, often emptying into the **moat**.

Machicolation An overhang above a gateway or at the top of a tower with holes through which guards could shoot or drop hot sand on attackers below.

Mantlet A wooden shield on wheels.

Melee A mock battle played during **tournaments**.

Moat A dry or water-filled ditch surrounding a castle.

Multure A fee charged by the lord to farmers for using his mill to grind grain.

Murder hole An opening in the ceiling through which defenders fired or dropped missiles on enemies below.

Oubliette An under-floor dungeon reached by a trapdoor.

Siege tower A wooden tower on wheels, which attackers used to climb over castle walls.

Trebuchet A powerful siege weapon like a large catapult.

Tournament An event where knights showed off their skills at jousting and in mock battles.